"*I have retained John to speak several times with different audiences. On each occasion he takes the time to seek my input for the desired outcome of the meeting. He adjusts his presentations accordingly and relates to the audience with practical, easy to implement suggestions.*"

Dennis J. Manning, CLU, ChFC
President & CEO,
Guardian Life Insurance Company

Written to John directly..."*In the years I've known you I have never seen your insights, strategies and process be as focused and valuable as they are now. Your thoughts, comments and philosophy are TIMELY.*"

Donald J. Faughnan
Faughnan Financial Network, Inc.
New York, NY

"*John Curry is an insightful and powerful advocate. He brings over 30 years of real field experience and wisdom to the table. His thoughts and observations are always on point and useful in many day to day situations we all encounter. John has an easy, southern gentleman style that makes the learning even more fun.*"

Joseph H. Guyton, Senior Associate
The Bulfinch Group
Lynnfield, MA

"The studied, measured, professional presentation of your seminar and the appreciative response it got from the participants bespoke all the continuing education you continue to do and your natural sincerity."
Joel G. Daunic
Financial Representative
Guardian Life Insurance Company
Gainesville, FL

"My personal thanks for your great presentation on our panel at The American College's Knowledge Summit. It was also delightful to get to know you. You bring integrity, knowledge, common sense, and passion to the business."
Susan D. Waring, CLU, ChFC
Executive VP and CAO-Life, VP Health
State Farm
Bloomington, IL

On preparing for a secure retirement... *"I wanted to thank you for your wonderful presentation at our Leader's Club in San Diego. Monday is our key day, which is why I had you front and center. You did a fantastic job. You educated, inspired, and motivated the audience. I may even 'liberate' your tape measure story. I hope you don't mind."*
David E. Nelson, MSM
Former VP, Agency Distribution &
Development Guardian

Preparing For A

SECURE
Retirement

Expert insight and advice
on implementing
The Secure Retirement Method

John H. Curry

Cover Design: Marjorie Schoelles
Edited and composed by: Marjorie Schoelles
MsXmedia.com (850) 294.9995

ISBN 978-0-9908714-0-8

Published & Distributed by: John H. Curry
P.O. Box 3892, Tallahassee, FL 32315
(850) 562-3000
Email: John@JohnHCurry.com
Web: www.JohnHCurry.com

Dedication

Many thanks to my wife Pat for your support all these years. To our children, Terri and Michael, and our grandchildren, Shelby, William, and Michael Jr.

To my staff and associates at North Florida Financial Corporation, especially Arlie Watkinson and Lee Harrison. Arlie for seeing the potential in a 22 year old who was loading milk trucks and going to school. Lee for the ongoing coaching and guidance. I thank you for your support and friendship.

To my clients. It has been a pleasure to work with so many families and businesses since 1975 to help provide financial peace of mind. Thank you for your trust and loyalty.

OVERVIEW OF THE SECURE RETIREMENT METHOD™

The Vision Session

You begin exploring your current situation and new possibilities for your future.

The Discovery Session

A detailed assessment and analysis of your current financial situation and a baseline to build on.

The Strategy Session

A step-by-step planning process to develop strategies, choose tools, and build a team to achieve your goals.

The Implementation Session

A system of tools, resources, capabilities, and expertise for effectively implementing your plans.

WHAT'S IN IT FOR YOU?

The program helps you protect your wealth, while choosing the best options for a secure retirement. The Secure Retirement Method™ helps you preserve and enhance your lifestyle, while achieving your retirement vision.

WHO SHOULD PARTICIPATE IN THE SECURE RETIREMENT METHOD™?

Anyone who is serious about planning their retirement. Participants who have already done significant work on their planning will enjoy working with professionals to give their planning package even greater clarity, depth, and creativity.

If you are starting from scratch, you will appreciate how the process accelerates the development of your planning.

Whatever your situation, we're confident you will find The Secure Retirement Method™ a valuable contribution to your future.

THREE <u>FREE</u> WAYS TO GET STARTED:

1. *The Secure Retirement Vision Session*™ This is your opportunity to build and protect your wealth, while choosing the best options for your secure retirement. During this session we will begin to explore your current situation and the new possibilities for your future. **Call today to schedule your complimentary session.**

2. *Strategies for Financial Success*™ *Newsletter*
Receive this monthly newsletter sent directly to your email. The newsletter contains valuable and useful information.

3. *The Secure Retirement Method Workshop* ™
To experience one of our workshops, call to find out when the next one is scheduled.

Flip to the next page and complete your **FREE** *scorecard!* ⟶

THE SECURE RETIREMENT SCORECARD™

NAME: _____ DATE: _____

Decide where your position is on the scale from 1 (disagree with statement)
to 10 (completely agree with statement).

1	I have a clear, well-defined vision of my future	1	2	3	4	5	6	7	8	9	10	
2	I have clear retirement goals	1	2	3	4	5	6	7	8	9	10	
3	I have a strategy to grow, protect my wealth, and optimize my retirement	1	2	3	4	5	6	7	8	9	10	
4	I have a step-by-step action plan to achieve my retirement goals	1	2	3	4	5	6	7	8	9	10	
5	My finances are organized and efficient	1	2	3	4	5	6	7	8	9	10	
6	I am confident about the performance of my investments	1	2	3	4	5	6	7	8	9	10	
7	I have a single source of trusted advice and I am able to make informed decisions	1	2	3	4	5	6	7	8	9	10	
8	I have a trusted team of professionals helping me achieve my goals	1	2	3	4	5	6	7	8	9	10	
9	I have a plan to protect and enhance my lifestyle	1	2	3	4	5	6	7	8	9	10	
10	I have a strong sense of confidence about my future	1	2	3	4	5	6	7	8	9	10	
	ADD COLUMN TOTALS											Your Score

John H. Curry, CLU, ChFC, AEP, MSFS, CLTC: Registered Representative and Financial Advisor of Park Avenue Securities, LLC (PAS) 3664 Coolidge Court, Tallahassee, FL 32311. Securities products/services and advisory services are offered through PAS, a registered broker-dealer and investment advisor. 1.850.562.9075. Financial Representative, The Guardian Life Insurance Company of America (Guardian), New York, NY. PAS is an indirect, wholly owned subsidiary of Guardian. North Florida Financial Corporation is not an affiliate or subsidiary of PAS or Guardian. Neither Park Avenue Securities, Guardian, nor their representatives render legal or tax advice. The Living Balance Sheet is a registered trademark of The Guardian Life Insurance Company of New York, NY.

PAS is a member FINRA, SIPC.

Table of Contents

Left: John Curry speaking at a gathering of Guardian professionals in San Diego.

Below: John with his wife Pat and grandson Michael at Walt Disney World®.

Who is John Curry and North Florida Financial Corporation?

I would like to give you a little background of who we are. Our firm is North Florida Financial Corporation, we represent the Guardian group of companies, and we offer investment advice and products through Park Avenue Securities. We don't give tax or legal advice.

You see a lot of letters after my name:

CLU – Chartered Life Underwriter
ChFC - Chartered Financial Consultant
AEP – Accredited Estate Planner
MSFS – Master of Science in Financial Services
CLTC – Certified Long-Term Care

You can read my bio for more detail but you should know that I have invested thirty-three years of my life in the business of helping people with retirement planning and financial planning. I started September 13, 1975. I am motivated to help individuals, business owners and people in the Florida Retirement System because my grandfather and my father both retired from the State and they did not get good information; they were left on their own and sold products. Some of the products were good and some of the products were bad and that's why I have such a passion for helping people prepare for a secure retirement.

John out on the lake with his dad.

What Would You Like to Accomplish?

Can you picture yourself here?

What would you like to accomplish? Time freedom and money freedom? I will share information that will help you make better money decisions. I will give you a lot of information in our short time together in this book.

I like to live by the Rotary "Four Way Test". First is it the *truth*? Second, is it *fair* for all concerned? Third, will it build *goodwill* and *better friendships*. And fourth, is it *beneficial* to all concerned? My philosophy is "do the right thing". I have some questions for you—if you learn new information that will challenge your old paradigm what will you do with that information? Will you embrace it or will you push it away?

One weekend, a bridge went out on Highway 267 between Highway 20 and I-10 near my lake house. A friend told me the bridge was out. Now, I could have driven all the way around (17 miles) to check it out or I could take his word for it. I know him and trust him; he is not a practical joker so there is no reason for me to waste my time driving all the way around and have to turn around and come back and go another way. Do you agree or disagree? If I didn't know the person or if the person had a tendency to stretch the truth or lie or have fun with people at their expense, I might be willing to drive over and check it out. On the other hand, I don't see bridges fall down very often so maybe I would drive over out of curiosity, to learn something. It's the same way with money decisions. Who is giving you advice? Do you know them? Do you know what they stand for? Check them out. If they are unwilling to give you information that should tell you something. You have the right to know. Consider these seven common planning mistakes that most people make when planning for retirement.

What is Your Vision of Retirement?

What is your vision of retirement? How do you feel about retirement? For some people retirement means being stuck, not being able to do the things they want to do. For other people, retirement means freedom.

There are two types of freedom—time freedom and money freedom. When you're working you don't have much time to do the things you want because you're trading time for money. Hopefully, when you retire it is just the opposite. Now you have money coming in that buys you time to do the things you want to do. Does that make sense? If you think it through, most people don't plan for retirement properly. The first question you should ask yourself is "what is my lifestyle going to look like in retirement"? How do you feel about retirement?

Time and money are a recurring theme. Uncertainty makes us think ahead and do some planning. Going in a different direction could mean a new career path. Pursuing other interests means there has to be some goal setting. My grandfather retired with forty plus years from the State of Florida, Department of Transportation; he had no interests other than hunting and fishing. He didn't live very long after retiring. My grandfather was a very physical man all of his working career working on bridge crews and construction but after retiring he became very inactive and died too soon. He didn't have 'things' ie. goals, to keep him going in retirement. He probably should never have retired.

This is one of my visions of retirement...what about you?

John fishing with his grandson.

Declaring Your Independence

"In 1776, fifty-six men signed a document to declare our independence…

… have you declared *your* financial independence?"

John H. Curry

In 1776, fifty-six men signed a document to declare their independence. What am I talking about? The Declaration of Independence. What does the Declaration of Independence have to do with you and financial planning? It has everything to do with it because the question is "have you declared your financial independence?"

Have you signed your documents declaring your financial independence? What are some of those documents? I'm talking about wills; trust provisions, health care directives and living wills. Life insurance, Long Term Care insurance and medical insurance are documents that provide financial independence. Most of us talk about these documents but don't follow through. Many people get good information but don't follow through and implement what they learn.

There are three phases to your financial independence:

Wealth Building
Wealth Distribution
Wealth Conservation

You have to build wealth so that you can enjoy it for the rest of your life (distribution). What happens to your wealth when you die? Who gets all of your stuff? That's what wealth conservation is. Who do you want it to go to? Corporations such as hospitals, nursing homes or the IRS in the form of taxes such as estate tax, capital gains tax, income tax, and gift tax? You have control over that, actually you have a lot more control than you realize.

What are the dangers to be eliminated? What are the opportunities to be focused on and captured? What are the strengths that you already have that you should reinforce and maximize? You have all three and no matter what your age, the dangers should be reduced or eliminated. There are things that could happen to you that could destroy your retirement financial plan and your family's security.

Don't let unanswered questions weigh on your mind!
List your 5 top risk factors on the next page.

What are your top 5 risk factors?

1. _____

_____

2. _____

_____

3. _____

_____

4. _____

_____

5. _____

_____

The Seven Common Planning Mistakes

Underestimating life expectancy: Almost everyone will live longer than they think they will. There are tremendous changes in technology that allow us to live longer. Some of us will live to be age 100 or older.

Paying too much in taxes: Almost everyone is paying more taxes than they have to. It is up to you to do something about it not the government.

Ignoring Inflation: Inflation is a silent thief—you expect the taxman to come after some of your money but you don't think about inflation, and it really takes money away from you; probably more than you realize.

Relying on government and employer retirement plans: This is a problem and it is getting bigger. We can no longer allow ourselves to be dependent on these plans. We must save money and create our own security.

Health care expenses and long-term care: Some people's entire paycheck goes to cover health insurance—

unbelievable! I see people who are retired and their prescription medication bill is greater than their mortgage payment ever was. This is a big problem for retirees.

Not saving enough money: Most of us don't save enough money. It comes down to personal responsibility. We must form the habit of saving money.

Buy financial products instead of a strategic plan: Many of us are guilty of buying a product because a friend said we should or a sales person pushes us to buy a product. If it doesn't look right, doesn't feel right—don't do it. If the product can't be verified to your satisfaction that you're going to be better off by acquiring that product then don't buy it!

Go to: www.JohnHCurry.com/7mistakes to sign up for your **FREE** report that contains more expert advice on avoiding the **Seven Common Planning Mistakes**. Prepare today for securing your retirement of tomorrow!

Four Financial Risks

There are four financial risks that everyone faces.

Number one is **dying too soon**. In the event you die today, would anybody be hurt financially because of your death? Do you want to leave behind a financial legacy?

Number two, **living too long**. Is it possible to live too long? What does living too long mean? Outliving your money. What happened in 2000, 2001, 2002 and 2008, 2009 with the stock market? Can you imagine going in to retirement and losing 30% to 40% of your money? How do you feel about retirement now? What about the stock market today? Some advisors just say "go back to work, no big deal" or "don't worry about it, you lost some money just move it back over to guaranteed accounts". Now you are stuck getting one or two percent to live on. We have short memories and take the attitude that won't happen to me when I retire. How do you know that? I'm pretty good at what I do and I have no idea what dangers are ahead of me. All I can do is plan the best I can today.

Number three is **becoming disabled** while working or in retirement. What happens when you become disabled and you need long-term care? You could wipe out a lifetime of savings.

I was at a benefit for caregivers of people who have Alzheimers—there were several people attending the event and a lot of money was raised. So many people are impacted not only emotionally but also financially because they become disabled in retirement. If you become disabled while you are working, you know you are in trouble because your paycheck stops. Most of us don't think about long-term care issues. This is important because everyone, in all likelihood, will be a caregiver at some point. Long-term care is a powerful issue and it can be devastating.

Number four is the need for **cash for an emergency or opportunity**. Who hasn't been financially embarrassed at some time in their lives? An emergency or an opportunity has come up and you don't have the money. You can make sure you don't have this problem by saving money on a regular basis. It doesn't matter so much the rate of return as the habit of saving the money. Sometimes we are happy to get <u>any</u> percent in the stock market.

How do you prepare for these Four Hazards?
I suggest you consider life insurance as a strategy. For more details download my FREE report, "Why I Like Life Insurance" at www.JohnHCurry.com/life

For 99% of human history, the average life expectancy was under 18 years of age

2/3 of all humans that have reached the age of 65 are alive today.

(Vierck, *Factbook on Aging, 1990*)

In 1900, average life expectancy was 47 years.

In 2005:

Male – 75.2   Female – 80.4

United States Life Expectancy Table 2005, data released September 2007 from
http://www.cdc.gov/nchs/products/pubs/pubd/hestats/prelimdeaths05/prelimdeaths05.htm

11

70 Million People in the United States will be 65,

or

20% of the population.

CSA Designation Training Course 2004

12

These slides are pulled from John's presentations to groups about the trends in aging and the impact of the future of secure retirements. For more information on the schedule of seminars or to inquire about having a presentation for your organization, please contact us at: www.JohnHCurry.com

Trends In Aging

For ninety nine percent of human history, the average life expectancy was under 18 years of age. Two thirds of all humans that have reached the age of 65 are alive today. What does that say about our society? We are getting older. What kind of impact does that have on our society? In 1900, the average life expectancy was 47 years. In 2009, the mortality table states that a male could expect to live 74 years and a female 79 years, so in a hundred years our life expectancy has gone from 47 years to 77 as an average. In the future, life expectancy is expected to be 100 years. Some scientists say 120 to 130 years.

Did you know that by 2030, an estimated seventy million people in the US will be 65 years old? That is twenty percent of the population and that is not just in the US. Japan, Australia, Canada and other countries have these same issues especially those in the baby boom era. By 2030, an estimated one million people in the US will be over 100 years of age. There was an article in the "Sarasota Times" in 2004, about a very active, spry 107-year-old woman that looked forward to going to a senior center three times a week.

From 2000 to 2030

The number of people aged 80 years or older in the United States will double to 19.5 million.

Centers for Disease Control and Prevention. Public health and aging: trends in aging—United States   13
and Worldwide. MMWR Morb Mortal Wkly Rep 2003;52(6):101-6.

Happy 100th Birthday!

Hallmark has a birthday card for age 100. It reads "It's time for one hundred good wishes, it's time to salute you because the world has been blessed for ten decades of you so sit back and enjoy the applause—congratulations on 100 wonderful years." Some of us, and I hope I am one, will live to be a 100. I hope someone sends me one of those cards.

We all have our thoughts about retirement—I have another card for retirement that reads, "So, what are your accomplishments? Enjoy your new found freedom and always remember what a difference you made in those whose lives you touched." So, enjoy your new found freedom but what about the difference you made in other people's lives? That's part of it too. We touch a lot of people's lives while we are here—how are we impacting those lives?

The key to longevity is avoiding rather than surviving disease. There is a great book that I would recommend you read it's called "Living to One Hundred"*.

*Check out the life expectancy quiz at: www.livingto100.com**

The referenced material is for educational purposes only and does not necessarily address the financial objectives, situation or specific needs of any individual investor. While the information contained herein is believed to be reliable, we cannot guarantee its accuracy or completeness.
Please note that individual situations can vary, therefore the information should be relied upon when coordinated with individual professional advice.
An RR of PAS, may not endorse, refer or promote a book. An RR of the Broker/Dealer promoting a book which recommends that clients not diversify assets and transfer security assets for life insurance is not acceptable
The information and views contained in these materials are for informational purposes only and do not contend to address the financial objectives, situation or specific needs of any individual investor. The information presented does not constitute, and should not be construed as, investment advice. Neither Park Avenue Securities nor (name of RR) provide tax or legal advice. Please consult your advisors regarding your specific situation. These materials are not presented or endorsed by Park Avenue Securities, The Guardian Life Insurance Company of America or any affiliated companies.

* Neither Guardian nor PAS has reviewed or approved the above referenced publication. As such, neither Guardian nor PAS recommends or endorses it in any way.
**Note regarding external links: Links to other sites are for your convenience in locating related information and services. This Agency, The Guardian Life Insurance Company of America (Guardian) and Park Avenue Securities, LLC (PAS) do not maintain these other sites and have no control over the organizations that maintain the sites or the information, products or services these organizations provide. Although this Agency, Guardian and PAS believe that the information from these organizations is reliable, we cannot guarantee its completeness or suitability for any purpose. Accordingly, this Agency, Guardian and PAS expressly disclaim any responsibility for the content, the accuracy of the information or the quality of products or services provided by the organizations that maintain these sites. This Agency, Guardian and PAS do not recommend or endorse these organizations or their products or services in any way.

Women and Aging

Ladies I don't want to pick on you but aging is definitely a woman's issue. When you look at what statistics show us, we find that women spend more years disabled and living in nursing homes longer; and they are more likely to be impoverished. Did you know that seventy five percent of seniors below poverty level are women, especially minorities?

Gentlemen, this is a problem! A lot of times, men have not done a good job financially of providing for their families whether it be life insurance, disability, long-term care, etc. My grandmother died at age 94, she was in a nursing home for almost eleven years. That is an unusually long period of time. When I would go to visit her most of the people I saw were women—very few men— because they had died and their wives were left behind.

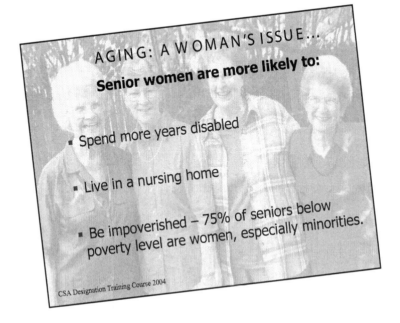

AGING: A WOMAN'S ISSUE...
Senior women are more likely to:

- Spend more years disabled

- Live in a nursing home

- Be impoverished – 75% of seniors below poverty level are women, especially minorities.

CSA Designation Training Course 2004

Long-Term Care

I know families where the adult children are fighting over taking care of their mother after their father died. Mom had taken care of their father until he died and now their mother needs care, and they are negotiating to provide so many hours to save money. They have a lot of issues.

Lets talk about long-term care insurance. If you can't afford long-term care for your spouse and yourself and you have to make a choice, I would take long-term care on the woman. Now, why would I say that? Because in all likelihood, the woman will be the caregiver of the man. Who will take care of her?

Long-term care is a catchall phrase. Long-term care

means extended care and typically care lasts longer than ninety days. Long-term care includes services for people who have lost the ability to maintain their independence.

There are three levels of care: skilled care, intermittent skilled care (may not be continuous), and custodial care.

Skilled care: This is care provided under a medical doctor's order by a licensed professional and the key word is "licensed" medical professional. It can't be your mom, dad, brother or sister it has to be a properly licensed person in their field. This does not include treatments that can be performed by non-medical personnel. Many people believe that their health insurance and medicare will cover long-term care expenses. They don't.

Custodial care: You've probably heard about ADL's (activities of daily living), bathing, toileting, dressing, transferring, eating and continence. Usually you will need two ADL's in effect in order for you to receive benefits under a policy that are generally not covered by Medicare. This represents ninety five percent of long-term care needs. This could be assisted living, skilled care, or in-home care. Who needs it? It could be needed at any age, however, the primary recipients are people who lose their independence due to aging, chronic conditions and disability.

What is Ronald Regan famous for other than being President? What was his illness? Alzheimer's. Alzheimer's, what a terrible disease. It is hard to imagine someone that great who at the end of his life didn't recognize his friends and family. We've experienced this with several of our clients.

Christopher Reeve, who played Superman, fell off a horse. All kinds of things can happen to us—car accidents, falling off a roof, etc.

What about Michael J. Fox? He has Parkinson Disease. How do you plan for these things? I can't promise you that you won't have a problem no one can. But you can plan and do the best you can TODAY.

Where does long-term care occur? Almost forty percent occurs in nursing homes. Five out of seven patients receive long-term care at home. Many people would prefer to be in their home for as long as possible when they have problems. Most people say they would like to stay in their home but that's where the care is the most expensive.

I have a friend who is paying $12 an hour for his mother-in-law, $12 an hour, twenty four hours a day, that's over $8,640 dollars per month going out and only half of that is covered with long-term care insurance, the rest is coming out of assets. They can't do that forever, the day will come when his mother-in-law will have to go to a nursing home because the nursing home is less expensive.

What are the costs of long-term care? The costs obviously vary nationwide, if you live in New York City you can expect to pay an average of $398 a day, in the Tallahassee area, about $202 and the national average is $209.* That is a lot of money, $202 a day for thirty days is $6,060 and $73,730 a year. Where will that money come from? You can pull $73,000 out of your retirement accounts or you can use long-term care insurance to cover it. Long-term care insurance is the best solution for most people.

Key Questions When Designing a Long Term Care Policy

What is the daily benefit to you? Do you want inflation protection or not, how long do you want to receive the

*Source:2008 Cost of Care Survey, Genworth Financial, March 2008

benefit? Do you want it to come in for your lifetime, three, four, five or ten years? How long are you going to use your money before you get the insurance company's money? If you have a lot of assets you might go with a ninety-day or one hundred eighty day waiting period. The longer the waiting period, the more of your money you are using to lower your premium but you will be spending your assets quicker.

Benefit Trigger

Earlier I talked about the activities of daily living and also premium; I suggest people get what their budget will allow. Don't wait to get the best plan because there is no "best plan" you get what you can afford at the time. Some people might say "I won't need it until I'm 65 or 70" but how will you know?

Long-Term Care Summary

As the average age increases we are going to need more long-term care. If you don't die until you're 80 or 90 that means you get "old". So if you don't die young and you get old and get sick you will need care . How do you pay for it? I talked about different levels of care—nursing homes, assisted living, skilled care and in-home care; these can all be devastating and require preplanning. Can you see how long-term care is part of retirement planning? What good is it to build up assets, a nest egg, your pension plan, 401(k), profit sharing plan, 403(b), and then lose it because you have to use it for long term care expenses in retirement? The very money you saved to take care of your family is taken away and transferred to whom? Corporations, nursing homes, hospitals and that's what you want to avoid.

For a **FREE** Report, "How to Use Long Term Care Insurance to Protect Your Retirement and Estate Assets", please visit: www.JohnHCurry.com/ltc

The Perfect Financial Storm

We are living longer. The baby boomers are the longest living generation so far. What's happening behind the baby boomers? A smaller generation. Is that a perfect demographic storm? Some people think so.

What about Social Security, Medicare, Medicaid, and pensions? What is happening with these? They are in trouble! There was an article in "Time Magazine", October 31st, 2006, that talks about "the great retirement rip-off"—they're talking about pension plans becoming underfunded and the Pension Benefit Guaranty Corporation trying to bail them out. Some people are concerned about what could happen in the public sector as well.

Just look at the number of news articles and reports regarding pension plans and 401(k) plans in the media today.

Challenges

What about interest rate risks, market risks and inflation? There are things that will take money from you. If you retire and you are too conservative you won't have enough income in retirement. There needs to be a balance between interest rates that are guaranteed and some money in the market to offset inflation but you've got to be careful. I don't want to paint gloom and doom and you rush out and say, "Oh my god, inflation is going to be so bad I've got to jump into the market and take risk". I'm not saying that at all.

I worked with a woman who put eighty percent of her money in a guaranteed interest account and only twenty percent in the market—why? Because she is ultra conservative. She said to me "John, the pain of losing some of my principle is much greater than my desire for gain in the market"—so as an advisor, what would you do for that lady? You put the money in something safe and secure so that her principal and her interest will not go away.

Someone else might say "well she's only going to get "X" percent interest". So what? If her fear is losing money then why should she put it at a high risk?

Ask yourself these three questions:

At what age would you like to retire?
At what age can you afford to retire?
What impact does long-term care have on your vision of retirement?

I love this quote:

"Experts estimate that in order to maintain your standard of living when you stop working you must replace seventy to ninety percent of your pre-retirement income". US Department of Labor

Where will that money come from? It is going to come from three sources: government such as Social Security, you, your savings and investment programs you've created and your employer 401(k) plan or pension plan. Most people today, don't have a pension plan.

What are you doing to coordinate your sources of retirement income?

Have you created your own private guaranteed retirement income plan?

FINANCIAL ILLITERACY

- Spiraling Debt
- Growing Bankruptcies
- Low Savings Rate
- Lack of Preparation for Retirement

Financial Illiteracy

Let's address financial illiteracy. What's happening out there? Spiraling debt, growing bankruptcy; so much so that Congress stepped in to do something about it.

You're probably aware of the low savings rate in the United States. According to the U.S. Department of Commerce from 2001 to 2007 the savings rate ranged from -0.1% to 4.2%. In 2008 it jumped to 8.2%.* Was this increase due to the fact that people were worried about the economy and started consuming less and saving more? Some people save a lot but the majority of people don't and they lack in their preparation for retirement..

*Bureau of Economic Analysis, percent of DPI, FFAs 2005

THE SECURE RETIREMENT METHOD™

Your Retirement Vision

4 questions?

1. Think ahead to the day of your retirement. Looking back from that day what has to have happened along the way for you to feel happy about retirement?

2. What obstacles and concerns stand in your way to achieving your vision of retirement?

3. What are the most important actions you must take to overcome these obstacles and concerns?

4. What progress have you already made toward achieving your retirement vision?

Getting Prepared for Retirement

What does retirement mean to you? What is your retirement plan? For some folks its winning the lottery—you go down and buy a lottery ticket and you expect to win. For some people that's their investment plan, that's their retirement plan.

Everyone has his or her view of retirement but it comes down to freedom—freedom in time and money. Some people are of the mindset that they can't wait until they retire—they want to retire and not go to work anymore, do nothing. I had a gentleman that retired at age 57 and I was giving him a hard time "you're too young to retire" he is now 62. He was "cheating" us out of his knowledge and wisdom. We are losing leaders in corporations, State government, and charitable organizations; we're losing them and we need them. If you are going to retire, be a volunteer. Work at your church, work at a charity, do something.

Think of retirement as a **GAME**. If you're experiencing <u>growth</u>, personal growth, intellectual growth and you're happy, and you're <u>active</u> because you're healthy and you have <u>money</u> and you're <u>excited</u> about what you are doing. How do you feel about retirement now? Retirement takes on a different view.

GAME = growth, active, money, excitement

For some people, retirement is depressing. I had the pleasure in 1981, to do a series of workshops for General Electric in Daytona, they had people that needed psychological counseling six months to a year after retirement because they had done nothing throughout their careers except work, work, work. They were getting divorces in retirement. These were people that lived with the same person thirty or forty years and getting divorced and they couldn't understand why. What they discovered was, the men especially, did not have any hobbies or interests other than work. They would get up everyday, drive the same route to work, sit at their desk, do their work and go home. Their spouses didn't know them! It took time to learn each other again and that's the real world. It's not just the husband it's the same for the wife. The "Leave it to Beaver" family where the wife stayed at home and did the dishes—those days are long gone. How would you feel about retirement if your days were like that? Would you want to retire or keep doing what you're doing?

There are some people who might say "I'm not retiring, I don't think I'll ever retire, I want control. If I don't want to go to work today, I want that ability. If I don't like someone because they are rude or obnoxious I don't want to deal with them". If you have control of the rules of the game maybe retirement is different. Who says you have to do retirement the way everybody else does retirement? Change the rules to suit you, invent your own retirement GAME. What do you think about that? You can do it.

I've had people in corporate jobs, State, City and County government say "oh I can't do XYZ"—they are right, they can't. You have a job. Could you have a business on the side? Many people can. I was talking with a gentleman who is a fireman and he has a lawn care business; he earns more money in his lawn care business than he does working at his job as a fireman. I know another gentleman who's a deputy sheriff and he makes more money at his business than he makes on his job. No one says that you have to sit in front of a television on weekends; you have the right to go out and do other things to make money and to grow.

John talking about protecting your piggy bank.

Objectives

I read an article in US News and World Report "Seven Reasons Not to Retire, While Continuing to Work and Improve Your Health, Mental Sharpness, Even Your Marriage"*. Some people are doing such a poor job with their investments they have to work longer. There are other reasons to work longer.

What are our objectives? Our objectives are to make sure that you're building wealth and that you're protecting that wealth. People are trying to break into your piggy bank everyday—everyday "they" are trying to get in there and take money away—taxes, inflation, medical costs, interest rates, fees and more.

Protection

The objective is to **maximize** protection and **minimize** costs and most people do just the opposite—they don't have proper car insurance, liability, disability, medical, and disability income insurance. They don't have wills or the proper amount and type of life insurance.

*June 12, 2006

My philosophy is real simple when it comes to protection—**it should be as perfect as you can get it.**

I talked about Christopher Reeve and Michael J. Fox earlier; Christopher Reeve didn't plan to have an accident and Michael J. Fox didn't plan on having Parkinsons but it happened. If you have your protection maximized you're better prepared for <u>life's untimely and unplanned events</u>.

What if you have a car accident and you hurt or you kill someone and you only have $50,000 liability coverage on your car? You're going to be sued for more than $50,000. It's important to coordinate insurance coverage—car insurance, home and personal liability so if you get sued you're protected. Does that make sense?

Sometimes we're spending money to protect other people but we are not protected.

I love this quote from Thoreau:

"If you have built castles in the air your work need not be lost, that's where they should be. Now put foundations under them".

That's what protection is; it's protecting everything you've worked for. Why build all this money in a mutual fund or a CD and have it taken away because of a lawsuit? That doesn't make sense.

Savings

Let's talk about savings, specifically retirement savings. We want to increase the rate of return, reduce risks, reduce taxes and stay liquid. You can invest for income or growth and you can focus primarily on tax deferred strategies.

Social Security is something everyone wants to talk about and most people are concerned about it and don't think it will be there when they retire. I believe it will be there. I believe we'll have an income test and perhaps an older age to collect it.

President Franklin Roosevelt said:

> "We can never insure one hundred percent of the population against one hundred percent of the hazards of life but we've tried to frame a law which will give some measure of protection to the average citizen and to his family against poverty and old age."

What was he talking about? Social Security. Is that what it looks like today? No, it has been changed so many times.

Social Security has become an entitlement program, we think we are entitled to it and we get angry when the folks in Washington want to reduce our benefits. We say, "Wait a minute. I pay all of this money in taxes and I'll never get anything back"! Social Security wasn't designed that way. It was never designed to get the money we paid in, it was to take care of the people ahead of us.

You may not know that the full retirement age now is based on the year you were born. If you were born between 1943 and 1954, retirement age is now 66 to get your full benefit. If you're younger, it goes to age 67 and there has been some talk about changing the full retirement age to 70. The earliest you can collect Social Security is age 62.

Problems and Solutions

There are fewer workers to support Social Security and Medicare and taxes are increasing. I'm concerned about my grandchildren's future. What about lower retirement and health benefits? We are seeing a decrease in the number of workers to support Social Security recipients. In 1950, it was sixteen to one, in 2000, three to one and it has been projected that in 2030, two to one.* Something has to

* http://www.socialsecurity.gov/qa.htm

change and I don't care if you're Republican or Democrat it doesn't matter, something has to change.

"In 2030, walkers will outnumber strollers as 10 million baby boomers hobble into old age."*

It sounds like all of the baby boomers are going to get old and decrepit but that's not true. I was eating breakfast with a gentleman who is 64, I didn't believe him and I asked to see his drivers license! I thought he was pulling my leg. He looked like he was 53 or 54. I have a client who is 90 years old and he looks like he's about 70. All of this nonsense that we're falling apart in retirement is just not true. What is the importance of this? If we're going to live longer and we're healthier than the generation before us then it stands to reason that we need to manage our money very well. If not, we will outlive our money.

When you get your Social Security statement what do you do with it? Do you throw it in a drawer or do you start reading? Visit www.ssa.gov to learn more about Social Security.

* The Coming Generational Storm -by: Kotlinkoff & Burns

Understanding Personal Responsibility

Can you change your past? Maybe you saved a lot of money and maybe you spent a lot of money but does that really matter? It's behind you—maybe you've done little or no planning. For example, let's say you are 43 and plan on retiring when you're 62, that's about half of your past. If you do as well in the next nineteen years as you did in the past 43 years would you be happy? Most people aren't happy they are very dissatisfied.

Does it stop at 62? How long will you live? Let's say you live to be 90, that would be twenty-eight more years, so now, we're not just talking about planning from 43 to 62, we're talking about going from 43 to 90 and there's the fallacy in what we've been taught. What if you're the one that lives to be a 100 years old or 120, but you planned on dying in your 80's because that's what you've been told all of your life?

What if you had your money in a 401(k), DROP, deferred comp, 403(b), profit sharing, pension, etc. and all of sudden that money runs out and you don't have the resources? How would you like to guarantee that does not happen? Even though we're losing our pension plans you have the right to set up your own private pension plan with annuities. Annuities are good investments if you use them properly. A pension plan is a type of life annuity.

Go to www.johnhcurry.com to find a great reading list that I have compiled. I believe the better informed you are, the better armed you are to secure your future retirement. While there, check out my articles and other resources.

Savings and Investments

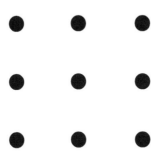

You'll find the solution to this puzzle toward the back of the book. Gotta keep you reading!

I have an exercise that I ask people to do—there are nine dots and the dots are to be connected with four straight lines, without removing your pen from the paper.

Go ahead, try it now. It is okay to write in the book. Keep reading for the solution (hint, check out the author info on page 84).

Tax Deferred Savings

You have tax deferred, tax-free and tax deductible savings programs. In tax deferred you have non-deductible IRA's, non-qualified annuities (non-qualified means you do not get a tax deduction up front). You have already paid the tax before you invested and when the money comes back to you in retirement you get pro-rated tax-free retirement income. Life insurance cash values are also tax deferred. You only pay taxes on the gain when you take the money out. If you take the money out with proper planning it's never taxed and that's exciting—no tax! A Roth IRA, grows tax free.

Tax Deductible Savings

People have expressed concerns about optional retirement plans like DROP. The DROP program comes under the heading of tax deductible. Anything you put money in with a tax deduction up front like deferred comp, 457 plans, 403(b) plans, 401(k) plans, profit sharing plans, etc. is a tax deductible plan. You can invest in mutual funds from this account or you can use programs like CD's and guaranteed interest annuities and variable annuties.

Two Types of Retirement Plans

Your Employer Plans

Pension or profit sharing plans come under tax deductible. There are two types of retirement plans: <u>defined contribution and defined benefit.</u> I like to tell this story about a kid and a business person buying ice cream. The business person went up to the counter and put $5 on the counter and said "I'd like an ice cream sundae", he never asked the price, he said "give me an ice cream sundae" and walked away eating his ice cream. A boy about 10 or 11 years old rides up on a bicycle and puts two quarters on the counter and says "I'd like fifty cents worth of ice cream in a cone please". Defined contribution was the kid with fifty cents, I only have fifty cents to contribute but I want as much as I can get for my money. The business owner says "I'm going to define the benefit that I want, I don't care what it costs just give me that benefit."

If you have a part-time business or you are in business now, you have the ability to design your own defined benefit plan and set aside money and you can have tax deductions.

What about defined contribution plans? That would be 401(k), deferred comp, the DROP, 403(b) plans, and the FRS Investment Plan. Your benefit is based on your contributions as an employee and how well the market does.

A defined benefit pension plan is based on a formula, your age, number of years of service and your income. All pension plans work that way. The employer makes contributions and the benefit is guaranteed for life. Unfortunately some plans are in trouble in the corporate world. More companies are freezing the pension benefits or closing the plans.

Retirement Systems

"In this chapter I explain a defined benefit pension plan by using the Florida Retirement System example. The concept is the same whether you have a corporate pension or a government pension. If you don't have a pension I can help you create one for yourself." John Curry

Defined Benefit Pension Plans

The Florida Retirement System

I like to talk about the Florida Retirement System (FRS) because I like for you to have a foundation so we can tie all of this together. I'm going to talk about John and Jane. They are 45 and 42. John is going to retire at 65 and Jane will be 62; you need both ages to calculate the benefits.

John's salary is $40,000 and we assume a three percent pay raise on average. John's average final compensation is projected to be $66,000 when he retires based on an average of his highest five years, not the last five but the highest five with thirty-three years of service.

John gets the maximum credit for each year, which is 1.68%. (33 years x 1.68% =55.44 %). If John were an elected officer or special risk or senior management it would be different. I'm talking about the State of Florida. This could be a County or City. This also applies to University, Community College or school district that has a guaranteed pension benefit program.

What are John's options? **Option 1** would be the maximum. John would get the maximum for life but upon his death Jane would get nothing. John's benefit is fifty-five percent of his average final compensation; $36,685. That's what John would be entitled to. We call that a "lifetime" pension.

Option 2 is a life income with ten years certain. John retires and gets an income for life. When he dies, what does Jane get? Jane gets ten years and that ten years starts when John retires <u>not when he dies</u>. The clock starts when you cash the first check. What if you go into DROP? John is in DROP for five years and dies what does Jane get? Five more years. You use up five years from DROP because you were retired when you went into the DROP program so only five more years are available. The factor is about ninety four percent of Option 1, $34,000, not a large cut to guarantee at least some income.

Option 3 is Joint Life with one hundred percent to the survivor. This is eighty four percent of Option 1 for $30,923. People choose this option because they want to take care of their spouse, they want an income for life and upon their death they want to make sure the spouse is covered. What happens when they both die? No more money, it dies with them.

Option 4 provides Joint Life and two thirds to the survivor, that's roughly ninety four percent or $34,000. What happens if Jane never worked outside the home and John took Option 4 what would Jane get? Jane gets $22,000. What if Jane dies first? John is reduced down to $22,000. No matter who dies first, the survivor is reduced to two thirds of the original amount.

Which option do you choose? How do you decide? If you are not married your choices are Option 1 or 2. You must have a dependant to take Option 3 or 4. A client had an adult child that was dependant upon her and she was going to take Option 4, I said "I don't think you want to do that" because the child in this case was 26 years younger—what would happen to her income? It would take a big reduction so in her case she took Option 2, She used life insurance to guarantee that, upon her death, money would go to a trust to support her child.

.

Retirement Payout Options

LIFETIME PENSION INCOME

LUMP SUM DISTRIBUTIONS

LIMITED PAYOUT PERIOD

Some people have the idea to take **Option 1**, lifetime income when they retire and have life insurance to guarantee an income to the spouse equal to Option 3. That's okay if it's done properly but it scares me a little because if you die early the family loses the income. They may have life insurance but they lose the ten-year certain income available under Option 2. I know of a case where the mother died in less than a year and the adult children lost a lot of money. If I had advised the family, I would have told them to take **Option 2**, and get life insurance because it would be a small risk to take to get an income for the ten year period. If you die along the way, whoever you name as your beneficiary gets the money. If you're single and are tempted to take Option 1, rethink that because there may not be a big difference between options 1 and 2. If you are extremely healthy and you're convinced you're going to live ten years or longer you may be willing to take that risk and choose Option 1.

What is the capitalized value of **Option 3**? If Option 3 is the option with a guaranteed level income of $31,000 and you could earn five percent interest on your money, you would need to have $618,000 dollars invested somewhere to give you that income stream, (31,000 / .05%=618,000).

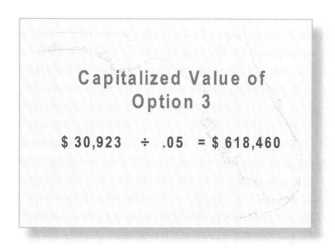

Capitalized Value of Option 3

$ 30,923 ÷ .05 = $ 618,460

At one of my seminars, I had a gentleman who had been a public servant say, "I don't have much wealth, I don't have any wealth really." I said, "wait a minute, you have a lot of wealth". Each of you, you and your wife, have your pension plan with the State of Florida that is the equivalent of well over $600,000 in both cases and that's $1.2 million; you can't get your $1.2 million in a lump sum but the income is the equivalent of $1.2 million invested. The problem is it doesn't show up on your balance sheet. It doesn't show up as being one million dollars. Wealth is either an income stream or assets. It can be cash, real estate, stocks or bonds but if you have an income stream that you can never outlive you've got to account for it somehow. Isn't that income stream worth something?

In this sample case, I suggested life insurance, to take care of his problems today, and that same insurance will assist him in retirement because he can walk into retirement with confidence and say "you know what? I'm going to take Option 1 or 2 because I bought life insurance years ago when I was younger to take care of my family, I'll use that now so I can take the higher pension option and when I die my family will be taken care of".

THE CHALLENGE...

HOW DO YOU CONVERT RETIREMENT ASSETS INTO LIFETIME INCOME?

Let's look at another scenario. The husband is putting money into the State deferred comp plan, $500 a month, $6,000 per year and the wife is putting money into a 401(k) that's being matched. They are putting some money into mutual funds. These funds were re-arranged in a manner to give them more benefits today and more income in retirement. They stopped their deferred comp for a while so he could increase his life insurance coverage. By putting this all together, this man was able to make better "macro" decisions.

POST-RETIREMENT RISKS

Longevity

Inflation

Health & Long-term care

Market: equity, volatility, interest rates, point-in-time

Family Issues

A Multi-Level Strategy

I am an authourized user of a service that allows you to have everything on your own personal web site. The web site is private and secure. I asked my attorney to send me a disk of my will, power of attorney, living will, healthcare directives, etc., to store on my web site. If I'm traveling and my house blows away in a hurricane, I can go to my web site and download copies of my will, insurance, etc.

Visit my website www.JohnHCurry.com and watch the 6 minute video.

That's what we are doing for our clients so they will have access to their information.

Check on Your Money

If you're retiring with $40,000 or $50,000 dollars a year it is like having a CD or investment account worth over a million dollars. If you had a million dollars in your bank account wouldn't you go down there occasionally and check on it? If someone had your money in a brokerage account or mutual fund or stock portfolio wouldn't you look at it? Ask them a few questions? You would check on it wouldn't you? But most of us don't do that when it comes to our retirement planning. We wait until the last minute and whatever we're shown that's what we take. Please, don't do that. You have the ability to do some planning today and to know what your options are when you retire.

Retirement Distribution Issues

There are some distribution issues that all of us face. At age 70 ½ we have to take money out under the required minimum distribution rule, (RMD). In 2016, baby boomers are going to start turning 70 ½ --what will be the impact on the market when that happens? Seventy-seven million baby boomers and lets pretend they are all 70 years old in 2016, and if they take out an average of a thousand dollars a month, just an average of a thousand, how much money will be coming out of the market? What's seventy seven million times a thousand? Seventy seven billion! What would be the market impact?

I share this with you to keep you thinking ahead. Don't just put all of your money in investments and leave it there—don't do that—those days are over. This buy and hold and just let it ride, I don't agree with that—you've got to do a little bit of planning from the standpoint of when you're going to retire. I'm talking about timing when you are going to retire—what will your lifestyle be like in five or ten years? Do you need more money or less money? You know that you're going to need money to live on, shift some of your assets to something that's more conservative, not all of it but some of it so you don't get hurt when the market does go down.

The Challenge

Here's a challenge for you—you're smart and you know you've got to save money and invest money; you don't need a financial advisor to tell you that. What you do need is someone that can help you convert your retirement assets into a lifetime income and help you coordinate everything. You are probably doing better than you think. When you get everything on your personal web page you can see it and understand it. You make better decisions. It's like a financial roadmap. I like to compare it to playing chess or monopoly—you've got to have a game board to know where you are and to understand how to play the game.

I believe people cannot really be financially secure or successful without considering important economic factors as they make their various money decisions.

Understanding the Real Cost of Living*

Overview

Life is More Than Math

Achieving personal financial success continues to be an elusive target for most Americans. Consumers of all income and net worth levels often express feelings of confusion, frustration, skepticism, and sometimes even fear as they approach the subjects of insurance and wealth management.

As a group, they find themselves suffering from the drag of numerous cost of living pressures which often lead to multiple unfavorable financial symptoms. For many, these factors remain a secret to them, and silently erode their protection, reduce their assets, increase their liabilities and inhibit their lifestyle.

In addition, most people operate with a relatively high level of <u>financial disorganization.</u> This is because a person's financial picture involves a host of insurance policies,

*The Real Cost of Living is produced and copyrighted by Guardian.

legal documents, employee fringe benefits, savings vehicles, debt instruments and securities products. People may be required to sift through mountains of information provided by a multitude of institutions and advisors in order to keep their affairs current. Many never accomplish a significant degree of organization and understanding of where they are financially. Those that do, typically only achieve it for an instant, and then drift off course again.

Guardian provides an innovative internet based platform that examines these 'real cost of living' factors, provides strategies to common financial symptoms, and creates instant organization by offering a wide angle view of a person's entire financial picture. It's an organizational tool forged from a philosophy that states that people cannot really be financially secure or successful without considering important economic factors as they make their various money decisions.

Financial Organization

When attempting to build a financial strategy, organization and easy access to a holistic view of one's current positioning are the missing ingredients for most people. Whereas personal financial information is typically scattered among multiple advisors, institutions, and accounts, I am an authorized user of a one-of-a-kind web-based platform which allows access to an entire financial picture from one location. Understanding how various financial pieces can be effectively integrated creates peace of mind and breeds a high level of financial confidence.

To keep abreast of ever changing financial circumstances, I am able to provide a personalized financial web home page for each client with an up-to-the-minute, interactive balance sheet of a person's protection portfolio, assets, and liabilities. All reports and cash flow strategies are then populated daily with information from over 6,000 financial institutions—and it can all be accessed from any computer—24/7. The ability to see and adjust finances from a private web page eliminates costly guesswork and allows users to become highly efficient in managing their finances.

Next, we offer a set of simple, logic based, financial game rules that if followed, will lead to improved results. People using their personalized web site are generally better protected, enjoy improved savings, more efficient management of debt and approach their finances with a clearer understanding of what their 'tomorrows' will cost.

Strategies are offered through conceptual vignettes and summary graphics designed to eliminate unnecessary number crunching. Rather than focusing on hard to predict financial goals or targets, **We stress the value of following game rules in the four Financial Domains of Protection, Assets, Liabilities, and Cash Flow.** Automated alerts can then be established, which trigger email reminders to monitor results and react to changing economic or life circumstances.

We understand that like life, long term financial needs are impossible to predict. In fact, it is the pursuit of a specific goal that often can get people off track. On the other hand, continual stress testing of products and strategies, so they can be counted on to deliver in all circumstances, is a much more important financial goal.

Real Cost of Living Factors

The primary strategies and products that make up a person's financial picture should be sustainable for decades into the future. Insurance programs must be designed correctly and built to last. Savings must be sufficient. Cash flow needs must fully anticipate what the world will feel like in the future. Liabilities must be manageable and efficient. The important answers to how much insurance, how much to save, and how much will be needed for retirement must reach beyond simple mathematical calculations and projections. The proper balance between lifestyle, protection, and saving for future goals is made both visible and attainable.

This is because people, money, and life have very little to do with math. Far more critical are the economic based, wealth eroding factors that make up a person's Real Cost of Living. These factors begin with inflation and income taxes, but also include other forms of taxation, the impact of new inventions, the cost of replacing products that have worn out, responding to fashion trends, unpredictable financial markets, and coping with the surprises of everyday life. It is only in the context of these real life economic variables that sound financial decision making can occur.

Many other planning systems make recommendations that rely on fragile assumptions and predictions, are based only on minimal needs, and ignore critical economic forces. They often focus on only one financial objective or one product at a time, failing to recognize the interdependent nature of every financial strategy across all four critical domains. By comparison, we introduce a complete set of unique Economic Observations vignettes to drive the point home that the future is very much unpredictable, and create ample motivation to become better organized, and also retrieve instant financial feedback in the context of these changing economic forces.

The Cost of Living Story

To put all of this in context, consider the following. Over the past decade, would you say that inflation has been high or low? Have marginal income tax brackets gone up or down? You would be correct, if you answered that inflation increases have been low and that income tax rates have actually fallen. In spite of these facts, people today are feeling greater financial pressure than ever before.

Question—How can it be that people feel the weight of increasing financial constraints in spite of an extended period of low inflation and lower income taxes?

First, it should be understood that <u>low annual inflation rates over the long run can trigger a significant loss of purchasing power</u>. For example, just 3% annual inflation for 30 years steals more than 50% from one's spending power. The cost of utilities, groceries, gas, college tuitions, cable TV, car repairs, vacations, home maintenance services, health care, and the like continue to creep upward due to the ongoing impact of inflation.

Of course there is the <u>income tax on earned income</u>, but many financial products also lead to additional costs as interest and earned dividends compound inside certain products. But income taxes alone don't tell the whole story as other taxes like state taxes, local taxes, sales taxes, property taxes, social security taxes, and Medicare taxes may increase the combined impact of taxation to 50% of gross income.

Now, think for a second about all of the <u>new products and services</u> that didn't even exist a few short years ago. Things like Plasma TVs, IPODs, cell phones, computers, cars that park on their own, GPS systems, satellite radio, laser printers, digital cameras, BlackBerrys, DVD players, MP3 players, X Box 360, PS 111, and on and on. In addition, health clubs, personal trainers, spa treatments, improved medical care, concierge treatment, dining, and travel all offer expanded levels of service compared to the past.

Another cost of living consideration involves the everyday <u>wear and tear on the products we already own</u>. Cars, tires, curtains, clothes, carpets, furniture, roof tops, paint, air conditioning, hot water heaters, washers and dryers, linens and more are designed such that they must be replaced some day.

At the same time people naturally aspire to have <u>a better life in the future</u>. This translates into a bigger home, stylish wardrobes, jewelry, a nicer car, a country club membership, a vacation property, a boat, and so on.

Finally, there is the sudden impact of <u>unexpected life events</u>. A premature death or disability, a lawsuit, property damage, tax increases, market declines, 5 years of college tuitions vs. only 4, graduate school, weddings, divorces, parents who suddenly, or perhaps gradually become dependents, assisted living, living too long, or any combination of the above can affect even the best laid plans.

Many people may be suffering from inadequate protection, excessive or poorly managed debt, low savings or poor cash flow design strategies, and find themselves behind as they prepare for retirement. Blame for these symptoms can be largely based on the public's miscalculation of what it does and will cost to live.

It is the total impact of long-term inflation, all forms of taxes, new gadgets, things wearing out, and the potential for life's surprises that continually thwarts efforts to achieve financial objectives. The combination of these 'real life' economic factors continue to drive up the cost of living which creates great challenges for those attempting to live for today while also protecting and building their wealth. It is important to understand the reality of these factors and include them as part of your protection and cash flow planning.

Common Cost of Living Factors

Each of the following economic factors affects a person's ability to build and protect wealth. It is critical that you understand each and every one of these factors:
- Inflation
- Taxes
- New Goods and Services
- Product Wear and Tear
- Improved Standards of Living
- Unexpected Life Events

Common Financial Myths

You must now begin to understand how people get off track financially. Typically, the implementation of inappropriate products and strategies is the result of subscribing to certain financial myths. It is important to discuss these myths and illustrate why they may not be entirely true. Since you may already believe in these myths (often strongly), it is extremely important that you understand you don't have to be wrong in order to dispel the myths. It is a matter of discussing these myths in a non-confrontational manner that enables people to discover for themselves that these myths are flawed.

All of these issues will be fully addressed. You will be introduced to the dramatic wealth building and cash flow design engines which are built to measure whether these and other 'financial myths' are actually blocking you from achieving optimal results. You will also learn the value of interacting and collaborating with an advisor instead of merely being presented the 'findings' contained in a financial plan proposal. This spontaneous working relationship leads to better understanding of the financial principles that must be implemented and maintained in order to achieve real success.

However, at this point, let's examine each of these myths in detail. See if you can explain why these myths might not be so, and why they may block a person from realizing financial balance and success.

- **Myth #1**--"My money only needs to keep pace with inflation."
- **Myth #2**--"I will be in a lower income tax bracket at retirement."
- **Myth #3**--"My 401(k) plan creates tax savings, which can be spent or invested.
- **Myth #4**--"Compounding interest creates a financial miracle."
- **Myth #5**--"I won't need life insurance when I retire."

•**Myth #6**--"A 15 year mortgage costs less than a 30 year mortgage."

•**Myth #7**--"Disinvesting is the same as investing."

•**Myth #8**--"Rate of return on my assets is more important than regular savings habits."

•**Myth #9**--"My financial plan will meet all of my needs."

•**Myth #10**--"To get more protection, I must incur additional expense."

Common Unfavorable Financial Symptoms

The miscalculation of the cost of living and being sidetracked by the many financial myths can cause people to adopt shortsighted strategies which produce unfavorable financial symptoms. Chasing rates of returns, misunderstanding of expense versus investment, missing hidden expenses or ignoring their long-term impact and searching for that 'magical product' to cure all financial woes are all examples of this. People have been fed complex mathematical analysis by institutions interested in selling their products, rather than receiving a reliably sound, 'economic based' philosophy and road map. If not addressed correctly, these strategies may collide to create financial havoc for many unsuspecting consumers. The symptoms listed below are the most common results.

By using your personal financial web page, you and I will quickly identify your present financial condition. This will enable you to get on track and stay there.

It is not uncommon for several of these financial symptoms to be present. We will help you identify why this is so and develop strategies to improve the financial balance of your plan. These steps may create increased financial efficiency and help you defend against the impact of the Real Cost of Living®.

Common Financial Symptoms include:

- **Inadequate Protection**

- **Insufficient Annual Savings**

- **Unnecessary High Risk**

- **Low Overall Return**

- **High Debt Balances**

- **Ineffective Tax Strategies**

- **Not Living Within Budget**

There are other features and benefits that your customized web page provides to you. In addition to those already described above, please consider the following:

- An up-to-the-minute, live snapshot of 401(k)s, IRAs, stocks, bonds, mutual funds, pension accounts, and credit and mortgage balances from over 6,000 financial institutions.

- Innovative software that allows for storage of audio files such as last wishes for loved ones or recorded last will and testaments, trusts, medical records, passports, etc., as well as account numbers and accumulation of Frequent Flyer Miles.

- Highly protected maintenance of consumer information and personal website content through state-of-the-art security systems and procedures.

• Aggregation of financial data creates reports posting daily fluctuations in assets, liabilities, cash flow and protection in order to gain real time calculation of net worth.

• Offers "Human Life Value" and "Income Replacement" calculators to evaluate gaps in life and disability insurance coverage.

• Dynamic simulators offer redeployment Cash Flow Design options which are used to identify protection, wealth building, and wealth distribution opportunities.

Summary

This personilized web based platform was developed by The Guardian Life Insurance Company of America as a proprietary tool for its financial representatives. Protection, Cash Flow, Retirement, Investment, and Business modules create a comprehensive platform where virtually every aspect of a person's financial life can be designed and monitored.

Review of Key Concepts

Financial organization through the use of your personilized financial web page is one of the cornerstones of sound, holistic planning. By studying financial decisions across the four critical financial domains with up-to-date information, you can make decisions that will enhance your ability to grow wealth efficiently with proper protection.

The Real Cost of Living ®is different for everyone and is impacted by a wide variety of economic based and wealth eroding factors. These factors must be taken into consideration in order for sound financial decision making to occur.

Cost of Living factors include:

- •Inflation
- •Taxes of all kinds
- •New Goods and Services
- •Product Wear and Tear
- •Improved Standard of Living
- •Unexpected Life Events

There are financial myths that affect the way people see the world and make financial decisions. Helping you understand the realities behind these myths will allow you to make better decisions. The most common financial myths are:

- **Myth #1**--"My money only needs to keep pace with inflation."
- **Myth #2**--"I will be in a lower income tax bracket at retirement."
- **Myth #3**--"My 401(k) plan creates tax savings, which can be spent or invested.
- **Myth #4**--"Compounding interest creates a financial miracle."
- **Myth #5**--"I won't need life insurance when I retire."
- **Myth #6**--"A 15 year mortgage costs less than a 30 year mortgage."
- **Myth #7**--"Disinvesting is the same as investing."
- **Myth #8**--"Rate of return on my assets is more important than regular savings habits."

•**Myth #9**--"My financial plan will meet all of my needs."

•**Myth #10**--"To get more protection, I must incur additional expense."

Common Financial Symptoms include:

- **Inadequate Protection**
- **Insufficient Annual Savings**
- **Unnecessary High Risk**
- **Low Overall Return**
- **High Debt Balances**
- **Ineffective Tax Strategies**
- **Not Living Within Budget**

*The Real Cost of Living is produced and copyrighted by Guardian.

To schedule a FREE focus session in person or by conference call, please call 850-562-3000 or email John@JohnHCurry.com.

Contact Information
John H. Curry
3664 Coolidge Court
P.O. Box 3892
Tallahassee, FL 32315

Tel: (850) 562-3000   Fax: (850) 562-2921
email John@JohnHCurry.com
www.JohnHCurry.com

Dear Friend,

Thank you for sharing your time with me as you read this book.

I am a passionate advocate of protecting families and their futures through what I do. That's why I am writing this note inviting you to come in for a No Cost, No Obligation FOCUS Session.

In the Freee FOCUS Session we will talk about:

Your Future
Your Opportunities
Your Concerns
Your Uniqueness
Your Strengths

At the end of our 45 minute session we will both know if it makes sense for us to meet again. If yes, we'll schedule another appointment. If no, we'll part having had the benefit of clarifying your goals and future. A win for everyone, with NO RISK to you!

John

P.S. This session can also be conducted by phone / computer conference.

About the Author

John H. Curry, CLU, ChFC, AEP, MSFS, CLTC is a Senior Associate of the North Florida Financial Corporation. John has assisted thousands of people in Preparing for a Secure Retirement. These experiences led to his creation of the Secure Retirement Method™. John has been associated with the insurance and financial services industry since 1975.

John's extensive education and experience in financial services enables him and his team to provide top-quality service to his clients and other advisors. John frequently holds educational workshops and seminars on the subject of retirement planning and long-term care planning.

Professional Designations and Affiliations:
CLU (Chartered Life Underwriter)
ChFC (Chartered Financial Consultant)
AEP (Accredited Estate Planner)
MSFS (Master of Science in Financial Services)
LUTCF (Life Underwriters Training Council Fellow)
CLTC (Certified in Long Term Care)
Past President of Tallahassee Regional Estate Planning Council
Past President of Tallahassee Association of Insurance and Financial Advisors
Past President of Society of Financial Service Professionals (Tallahassee Chapter)

John is active in the Tallahassee Chamber of Commerce and a graduate of Leadership Tallahassee (Class 6), the Sunrise Rotary Club (Past President), the Marzuq Shrine and the Boy Scouts of America.

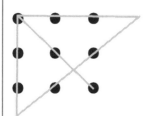 I connect the dots by going outside the nine dots. Did I follow the rules? Yes! Ever heard about thinking outside the box? That's what I've done. You don't have to do things the way everyone else does. It is ok to follow your own plan.
I can help you think outside the box.

Preparing for a Secure Retirement
Quick Order Form

Fax orders: (850) 562-2921. Send a copy of this form.

Internet orders: log on to: JohnHCurry.com/book

By mail: John H Curry
Attn: Book Fulfilment Department
PO Box 3892 Tallahassee, FL 32315

Order copies for friends and family members too!

Telephone orders: (850) 562-3000.

Name _____

Billing Address (must match credit card statement)

_____

City, State, Zip _____

Shipping Address (if different) _____

_____

City, State, Zip _____

Phone _____ Fax _____

Email _____

Quantity_____ x Price $19.97__ = Total _____

Applicable **sales tax** will be added. $5 shipping and handling.

☐ VISA ☐ Mastercard ☐ AMEX ☐ Check Enclosed

Credit Card Number _____Exp_____

Credit Card Code # _____ (VISA/MC - 3 digits on back, AMEX - 4 digits on front)

Full Name On Card: _____

Signature: _____Date:_____

Notes:

Notes:

Notes:

Notes:

Preparing for a Secure Retirement
Quick Order Form

Fax orders: (850) 562-2921. Send a copy of this form.

Internet orders: log on to: JohnHCurry.com/book

By mail: John H Curry
Attn: Book Fulfilment Department
PO Box 3892 Tallahassee, FL 32315

Order copies for friends and family members too!

Telephone orders: (850) 562-3000.

Name _____

Billing Address (must match credit card statement)

_____

City, State, Zip _____

Shipping Address (if different) _____

_____

City, State, Zip _____

Phone _____   Fax _____

Email _____

Quantity_____ x Price $19.97__ = Total _____

Applicable **sales tax** will be added. $5 shipping and handling.

□ VISA   □ Mastercard   □ AMEX   □ Check Enclosed

Credit Card Number _____Exp_____

Credit Card Code # _____ (VISA/MC - 3 digits on back, AMEX - 4 digits on front)

Full Name On Card: _____

Signature: _____Date:_____

Made in the USA
Columbia, SC
05 February 2019